Teacher's Resource Manual

Success in Science

BASIC BIOLOGY

GLOBE FEARON

Pearson Learning Group

Executive Editor: Barbara Levadi
Senior Editor: Francie Holder
Project Editors: Karen Bernhaut, Douglas Falk, Amy Jolin
Teacher's Resource Manual Editor: Linda Zierdt-Warshaw
Editorial Assistant: Kris Shepos-Salvatore
Editorial Development: WordWise, Inc.
Production Director: Penny Gibson
Production Editor: Walter Niedner
Interior Design and Electronic Page Production: Pencil Point Studio
Market Manager: Sandra Hutchison
Cover Design: Leslie Baker, Pat Smythe

ISBN 0-8359-1196-9
Printed in the United States of America
6 7 8 9 10   06 05

1-800-321-3106
www.pearsonlearning.com

CONTENTS

THE TEACHER'S RESOURCE MANUAL

This Teacher's Resource Manual contains the following:

- Guide to the Lessons

    This section describes the parts of the lessons in the student edition and provides approaches to teaching each part.

- Cooperative Learning Strategies

    This section provides general guidelines for cooperative learning activities.

- Teaching Strategies for ESL/LEP Students

    This section offers strategies for assisting ESL/LEP students with each part of the lesson.

- Unit by Unit Teaching Guide

    This guide contains unit opener connections, additional teaching tips for selected lessons, ideas for hands-on activities, and suggestions for student portfolios.

- Student Edition Answer Key

    This section contains answers to all questions in the student edition.

- Unit Tests

    This section contains brief assessments for each of the units in the student edition.

- Unit Test Answers

    This section contains answers to all questions in the unit tests.

GUIDE TO THE LESSONS

Each lesson in *Success in Science* contains the following parts: **Key Words**—new vocabulary and definitions, **Key Ideas**—a synopsis of the new information presented in the lesson, **Exposition**—the lesson text, **Take Another Look**—alternate summary of lesson information, and **Check Your Understanding** and **What Do You Know?**—evaluation exercises that allow students to measure their understanding of the lesson. The following suggestions provide alternate approaches for teaching each of these lesson parts. You may wish to use the **Practice Test** included in each unit as a diagnostic tool to determine students prior knowledge about a subject.

Key Words

Biology, like any scientific discipline, possesses its own scientific terminology. Becoming familiar with this vocabulary enables students to grasp ideas and exchange information with others. The teaching of Key Words and vocabulary development are important parts of all science teaching.

The Key Words listed and defined at the beginning of each lesson provide students with an overview of the information presented in the lesson. Key Words are printed in **bold** type at the place where they are used and defined in the text. A variety of exercises and strategies can be implemented to review the Key Words for each lesson. Some of these exercises and techniques include the following:

- Have students write a definition or a sentence using each Key Word prior to beginning the lesson. At the completion of the lesson, have students repeat this exercise and compare their responses.

- Create illustrated flash cards of each Key Word in the lesson. Introduce the lesson by showing the flash cards and asking students to define each term based on the illustration and their prior knowledge. Flash cards can also be used as a unit review of Key Words.

- Have students use a dictionary to find the meaning of each Key Word and record the definition. Then ask students to restate or rewrite each definition in their own words.

- Identify root words and prefixes that appear in the Key Words. If possible, establish a running list of these word parts on a chalkboard or a newsprint chart where they can be saved and easily observed by all students. Refer to the list of word parts as new words are introduced in each lesson.

Key Ideas

As with Key Words, the Key Ideas for each lesson provide students with an overview and an organization of the material presented in the lessons. Strategies for teaching Key Ideas include the following:

- Before reading the Key Ideas, assess students' prior knowledge by asking them what they already know about the lesson topic. Record student responses on the chalkboard. Review the responses after reading the Key Ideas.

- Ask students to read the Key Ideas aloud. Discuss the main information presented in each statement after it is read.

- Have students read the Key Ideas silently. Then ask students to rewrite the information in their own words or as an outline.

- When appropriate, show films or videos that relate to the topics presented in the lesson. In some cases, you may wish to have students watch television programs that relate to the Key Ideas.

Exposition

The information contained in each lesson is organized from simple to more complex and builds upon information as it is presented. Each lesson has an introductory paragraph followed by text divided into areas identified with subheads. Each block of text following a subhead can be studied independently. Students may feel less intimidated and anxious by breaking the lesson down into these smaller units. Periodically, in-text questions appear to provide students with an opportunity to assess their understanding of the basic concepts. In addition, the following strategies can be implemented while teaching the lessons.

- Have students work together in small groups (three to four students each) to read and discuss the parts of the lesson. Encourage students to write down anything they do not understand for further discussion.

- Ask student volunteers to read parts of the lesson aloud and then summarize the information in their own words.

- Working as individuals or in small groups, ask students to outline the entire lesson, including specific information and Key Words.

- Conduct demonstrations as appropriate to reinforce the material presented in the lesson.

- Provide ideas for cross-disciplinary activities that relate history, literature and writing, art, drama, social studies, health, and mathematics, to the topics being studied.

- Have students read aloud sections of the lesson identified by subheads. After reading each section, have a student volunteer create a concept map of the material on the chalkboard. Review the graphic as a class.

Take Another Look

This section of the lesson summarizes lesson information graphically through the use of charts, concept maps, or diagrams. The following strategies can be used in reviewing this section of the lesson.

- Reproduce the figure in this section onto an acetate, then project it over head. As you point to each section of the concept map, illustration, or chart, ask students to review what they learned in the lesson.

- Redraw the concept maps and/or charts on an acetate, omitting key information. For example, redraw the concept map with some of the key terms deleted. Use an overhead projector to show the revised figure to the class. Ask students to fill in the missing information.

- Ask students to summarize in paragraph form the information presented in charts and concept maps.

- Working in small groups, have students change the format of the figure in this part of the lesson. For example, ask them to change the information from a concept map into an outline or a chart.

Check Your Understanding

This section, at the end of each lesson, is designed to allow students to check their understanding of the material introduced in the lesson. Each review assesses knowledge in a variety of formats: understanding word relationships, labeling diagrams, fill-in-the-blank questions, and completing outlines and concept maps. This section tests basic recall of the main points as presented in the text.

What Do You Know?

This section allows students to go a bit farther in checking their understanding of the concepts presented. Questions here require writing answers in complete sentences. You might want to use the following strategies when teaching the Check Your Understanding or What Do You Know? sections of the lesson:

- Have students work in small groups to complete the exercises. One student in the group may want to read questions aloud to other students. Students should then review their answers as a group, consulting with the teacher on any answers of which they are unsure.

- Ask students to develop quiz games that include the information in this lesson. Students may organize competitions among individuals or teams of individuals to play the quiz game.

COOPERATIVE LEARNING STRATEGIES

Strategies for cooperative learning are very effective when teaching biology in classrooms having diverse populations. Pairing students who have strong science and mathematics skills or proficiency in reading and writing with students having weaker skills in these areas will lead to student success and enhanced understanding of the subject. Students are often more relaxed and feel more confident when working with other students rather than with a teacher or another adult. Also, having students work in groups allows them an opportunity to recognize and build upon individual strengths and develop an appreciation for cultural differences.

You may wish to follow the general guidelines indicated below when using cooperative learning strategies.

GROUP SIZE. Student groups can vary in size from two to as many as eight students. Smaller groups require fewer group experiences and skills to make the group function smoothly and successfully. First time users of cooperative learning strategies often find greater success with smaller groups.

OBJECTIVES. Each student in the group needs to know the expectations of the activity. Be specific in explaining the group goal: to demonstrate understanding of a new concept, to create a product such as a chart or report, to perform a skit, or to demonstrate a process. You may need to work with each group to make sure that all students understand the objectives and intended outcome of the activity.

INDIVIDUAL RESPONSIBILITY AND ACCOUNTABILITY. Each member of the group is responsible and accountable for the successful outcome of the assignment. Each group member is also responsible for the understanding and learning of other group members. You may need to work with each group to help students identify their individual responsibilities to the group.

POSITIVE INTERACTION. Successful cooperative learning occurs when all group members realize that participation and collaboration of all members is required for group success. Students must, as a result, learn to work and cooperate with one another and recognize one another's differences. An incentive for cooperation within the group may be assigning the same grade for each group member.

Suggestions for cooperative learning activities might include some of the following: planning, writing, and performing skits; making videos; conducting experiments; doing research projects with a report, chart, or notebook as a final product; holding debates; creating posters or classroom displays; making diagrams or models; conducting surveys; doing out-of-school research; taking field trips; and doing demonstrations for the rest of the class.

TEACHING STRATEGIES FOR ESL/LEP STUDENTS

Although the thought of teaching biology in a language diverse classroom may seem overwhelming, teachers should remember that techniques for teaching ESL/LEP students are simply good teaching techniques that are directed toward a student's special needs. The ESL/LEP population includes students for whom English is a second language and native English speakers with limited proficiency. With an awareness of what these students need and what works for them, teachers can easily adapt their instructional styles to language diverse classrooms.

Lesson Plans

1. **LESSON TITLE.** Organizes the thinking needed to learn concepts.

2. **KEY WORDS.** Consist of the terms required to learn the main concepts of the lesson. Learning the vocabulary builds the background necessary for understanding the lesson material.

3. **KEY IDEAS.** Focus and organize the learning process on the main reason for studying the particular theme or topic.

4. **PRE-TESTING.** Reveals if students have the background knowledge required for the lesson. If not, the teacher builds this background knowledge. This phase requires interaction and follow-up between the teacher and the class.

5. **EXPOSITION.** Includes all the activities the teacher does with students either in groups or as a class to provide the facts they need to begin the learning process.

6. **TAKE ANOTHER LOOK.** Creates interaction among students, between students and the text, and between the teacher and students to practice their growing knowledge of the concepts of the lesson. At this point, the teacher must monitor student progress and adjust the lesson accordingly.

7. **FOLLOW-UP ACTIVITIES.** Include independent activities in which students practice the skills they have developed throughout the lesson. These activities provide an opportunity for the teacher to assess whether the students are ready for their final evaluation. Writing exercises promote word and concept retention.

8. **EVALUATION.** Sets up demonstrations of mastery of the concepts. Evaluation activities need not be language based. They might include activities such as making a collage and role playing. The method of evaluation should match the stage of language development of the students.

Strategies

Effective strategies for developing and presenting lessons for ESL/LEP students include the following:

MODELING.   Visual examples used to explain what is expected.

CONTEXTUAL CLUES.   Use of real objects, pantomime, gestures, and connection of the familiar with the unknown.

BUILT-IN REDUNDANCY.   Repetition, paraphrasing, and restatement.

AGE APPROPRIATENESS.   Tasks reasonably difficult for the student's age.

HUMOR.   Spontaneous and planned to lower anxiety and increase chances for success.

EQUAL STATUS ACTIVITIES.   Two-way cooperative interactions between and among learners, such as peer tutoring and cross-cultural activities.

COOPERATIVE ACTIVITIES.   Structured techniques with positive interdependence and individual accountability.

Activities and Techniques

Experienced biology teachers working with ESL/LEP students recommend that students have a good dictionary. These teachers often provide basic word lists to be learned and memorized for automatic recognition. They provide an outline of the main ideas and simplify English to increase a students comprehension.

Teachers might consider these additional activities to implement ESL/LEP strategies:

- Summarize or paraphrase a paragraph or two, perhaps in the primary language. Then, have students translate to English, using a dictionary.

- Working in small groups with a student who is more proficient in English, have students summarize the key ideas in each lesson.

- Have students create visual displays: collages, posters, bulletin board displays, and so forth.

- Write down each of the steps of a particular process (such as mitosis) on a series of cards. In small groups, have students arrange the cards in the correct order.

- Write each sentence of a three-to-five sentence paragraph on separate index cards. In small groups, have students arrange the cards in the order that makes the most sense. Ask them to explain their arrangement.

- Create picture cards for the Key Words.

Unit 1

Unit Opener Connections

Explain that all organisms are made up of cells of different sizes and shapes. Using an overhead projector or individual microscopes, show prepared slides of the following cells: euglena; paramecia; amoeba; algae; bacteria; plant cells from roots, leaves, and stems; and human cells such as blood, nerve, epithelial, egg, and sperm. Point out the cell structures described in Lessons 2 and 3.

Teaching Tips

Lesson 1: Discuss how technology has led to greater knowledge about cells. Show the observable differences in detail resulting from use of a hand lens, binocular and monocular microscopes, and photos produced by electron microscopes.

Lesson 8: Draw the stages of mitosis on the board to refer to as you complete the lesson.

Hands-On

Have students half-fill a large bowl with clear water. Then have them put colored water into various membranous containers (balloons, various grades of plastic wrap, sandwich bags, etc.) and suspend them in the bowl of water. Observe where diffusion occurs. Follow the activity with a discussion of membrane permeability.

Portfolio

Item 4: Have references, such as high school or college biology texts, available for students to refer to when making their flow charts of photosynthesis.

Item 5: Circles of construction paper, paper clips, buttons, string, and pipe cleaners are examples of materials that can be substituted for making models of mitosis.

Unit 2

Unit Opener Connections

This unit opener works well with lesson 11. Show students pictures of children and adults. Ask them to "match" the children to the adults as if the children and adults were related. Ask students to explain why they paired children with specific adults. Students should indicate they matched children to adults because of common traits such as hair and eye color.

Teaching Tips

Lesson 9: Review with students what they have already learned about DNA and cell division. Remind them that DNA is a nucleic acid found in the cells of organisms.

Lesson 10: Emphasize that meiosis reduces the diploid number by half.

Lesson 11: Review that all traits of an organism are controlled by genes.

Hands-On

Have students conduct a survey of at least twenty family members and neighbors. Have students find out if siblings share the same traits such as eye color, hair color, and hair texture. Then have students compile their results into a large graph or chart to share with the class. Ask students to draw conclusions about their findings.

Portfolio

Item 3: Have references, such as college biology texts, available for students to use to research base triplets and the amino acids for which they code.

Item 7: Remind students that an important part of a doctor's job is to present information accurately and tactfully.

Unit 3

Unit Opener Connection

The unit opener works well with Lesson 15. Ask students if they have seen the movie, *Jurassic Park*. Encourage them to share what they learned about dinosaurs and their environment from the movie. Try to elicit possible connections between changes in the environment and the extinction of dinosaurs. Extend this discussion to environmental changes causing other species to become endangered or extinct.

Teaching Tips

Lesson 14: Be prepared to answer students' questions about the validity of evolution. Explain that evolution is a scientific theory. Review what a theory is and how it is validated.

Lesson 15: Many students have a great interest in fossils. Encourage them to share what they already know with others.

Hands-On

One adaptation of humans is the opposable thumb. Have half the students tape their thumbs to the sides of their hands so they cannot use them. Have both groups execute various activities that require grasping. Follow this activity with a discussion of how this adaptation provides selective advantage.

Students can make their own fossils using coins, shells, and other hard objects placed in plaster of Paris. Follow package directions for mixing the plaster of Paris.

Portfolio

Item 1: The June 1993 issue of *National Geographic* has an excellent article with photographs about the discovery of the Ice Man.

Item 2: Many museums require that group reservations be made well in advance.

Item 7: This could also be a good activity to incorporate as part of Item 2.

Unit 4

Unit Opener Connection

Use the Unit Opener with Lesson 21. From a local grocery store obtain a variety of mushrooms of different sizes, colors, and shapes. Many groceries carry white mushrooms, dried mushrooms, and wild mushrooms such as shitaki and portobello. Have students examine the differences and similarities among the mushrooms.

Teaching Tips

Lesson 17: Review the characteristics of living things. Tell students that the traits of viruses fit somewhere between living and nonliving things, but are important to other living things.

Lesson 18: Explain that bacteria and viruses can be both harmful and helpful. Ask students to describe ways in which bacteria and viruses are both harmful and helpful.

Hands-On

Using common household and craft materials, such as pipe cleaners, buttons, beads, and so forth, have students make models of round, rod-shaped, and spiral bacteria both individually and in chains and clusters if appropriate. Have students calculate how much larger their models are than actual bacteria of the same type.

Portfolio

Item 1: If done at school, the cafeteria may be able to supply the necessary ingredients and equipment to make yogurt.

Item 8: Provide students with thermometers and a variety of containers in which to grow the yeast. Use water directly from the tap; do no heat or cool the water.

Unit 5

Unit Opener Connection

Bring to class examples of the plants described in the unit opener (and others as appropriate such as spinach, cabbage, and asparagus). If possible, bring in growing plants rather than those purchased in the grocery store. As you read the opening paragraphs, have students observe and describe the plant parts identified in Lesson 23. At the end of the lesson, make a salad for the class.

Teaching Tips

Lesson 22: Students may not have seen living ferns or mosses. Obtain samples from florists or nurseries.

Lesson 23: From a local florist, obtain flowers of different shapes and sizes for students to compare.

Lesson 24: Show students seed pods of different sizes and shapes. Open the pods to expose the seeds.

Hands-On

Have students examine celery stalks. Vascular tissue is clearly visible. Cut off the ends of a stalk and place the stalk in colored water. Have students observe the movement of the water up the stalk. Follow the activity with a discussion of the role of vascular tissue in a plant.

Portfolio

Item 1: Students may need a letter of introduction to collect food examples at a local grocery.

Item 3: Ivy and philodendron plants are good substitutes to use here. They respond quickly to changes in light and water.

Item 4: Seeds such as beans, peas, radishes, and corn will germinate faster if first soaked overnight in water.

Unit 6

Unit Opener Connections

Bring to class examples or photos of spiders, beetles, and insects. You may be able to borrow specimens from a local college or museum. Encourage students to closely observe the examples and describe their similarities, differences, and characteristics as identified in Lessons 28 through 30.

Teaching Tips

Lesson 25: Review with students that animals without backbones are called invertebrates. Ask students for examples of invertebrates.

Lesson 29: Many students think all insects are "disgusting" and/or harmful. Provide numerous examples of how insects benefit humans and other living things.

Hands-On

Students can raise a number of invertebrates in the classroom. Work with local pet and tropical fish stores to obtain containers and supplies to maintain live invertebrates such as snails, clams, crawfish, millipedes, centipedes, starfish, and insects such as ants and honeybees. Assign responsible students to care for the live animals.

Portfolio

Item 1: Caution students who establish an ant farm to make certain that the ants cannot escape. You may want to make arrangements with the school cafeteria to obtain small amounts of food scraps to feed the ants.

Item 5: Hermit crabs are available at pet stores and from biological supply companies.

Unit 7

Unit Opener Connections

Ask students to name their favorite animals. Write their responses on the board. Then ask which of the animals have fur and which have four limbs (arms and legs). Tell students that these are two characteristics of mammals. Show students photos of a variety of mammals and point out the mammalian characteristics described in Lesson 38 such as hair, a distinct head and neck, and four limbs.

Teaching Tips

Lesson 32: Describe and show illustrations of the stages of life during which humans exhibit chordate characteristics such as gill slits.

Lesson 34: Prior to the lesson, ask students to describe what kinds of changes an animal would need to make to be able to move from life in the water to life on land.

Hands-On

Obtain various sized whole fish and fish skeletons from a local fish store. Have students observe the external characteristics as well as the gill slits. Have them carefully study the vertebrae and note how the size of the vertebrae is relative to the size of the fish. Discuss the significance of this in terms of support of the organism. Other vertebrates can be used, if available.

Portfolio

Item 3: Students may want to inquire about local bird-watching clubs and organizations. Many of these groups welcome visitors and gladly share information with beginners.

Item 6: Many natural history museums have educational programs for different levels of students. Inquire if the class can meet with a vertebrate paleontologist or if he or she can visit your class.

Unit 8

Unit Opener Connections

With student input, draw on the chalkboard the relationships among the organisms and the nonliving parts of the environment described in the unit opener. Include arrows that show how DDT was passed from one organism to another. Discuss the widespread impact of DDT on the environment and its eventual ban.

Teaching Tips

Lesson 39: Explain that all things on the earth, both living and nonliving, are related and connected to each other. Ask for examples.

Lesson 41: Point out different locations on a world map. Ask students to describe the environment and biomes of each area.

Lesson 42: Discuss with students what they can do as individuals to reduce pollution.

Hands-On

To demonstrate an ecosystem, have students set up one or more aquaria in the classroom. Provide gravel, fish, snails, and other small animals and plants. Have students observe and monitor the tanks over a period of several weeks. Ask them to draw food webs and energy pyramids relating to each tank.

Portfolio

Item 1: Remind students that an aquarium or a pond in a local park are small ecosystems.

Item 2: Have an almanac available as a resource.

Item 4: This is a good opportunity for cooperative learning. Encourage students to use their talents in art and construction to create costumes and props for the skit. In advance, set aside a date for students to perform their skit.

Unit 9

Unit Opener Connections

Have student volunteers act out the motions described in the unit opener. Ask students to identify which parts of the body, and which body systems if they know them, are involved in each motion. Encourage students to describe how the body parts or systems are coordinated and controlled. As you complete each lesson in the unit, refer to these motions and again ask students to describe the body parts and systems involved.

Teaching Tips

Lesson 43: If possible, show a model human skeleton to the class. Point out the different kinds of joints and the different sizes and shapes of the bones.

Lesson 44: You may want to dissect a cow heart as a demonstration for the class. Point out the parts of the heart and compare them to the human heart shown in Fig. 44-1.

Hands-On

Provide students with string, straws, plastic bags, hoses, and pipes to make a life-size model of the digestive system. Provide reference materials for students to use to determine the number of teeth in the mouth; the length of the esophagus, small intestine, and large intestine; and similar information. Make sure students label the parts of their models and describe the function of each part.

Portfolio

Item 1: Encourage students to also consider what kinds of protection they would need while traveling through the body.

Item 5: You may want to provide students with additional health texts and other books on the human body such as *The Incredible Machine* by the National Geographic Society.

STUDENT EDITION Answer Key

Unit 1

Lesson 1 The Cell Theory

1. Hooke observed thousands of small, walled sections in cork sections, which he called cells. **2.** Virchow stated that all cells come from other living cells. **3.** Protoplasm is a living material. **4.** d **5.** b **6.** c **7.** a **8.** A cell is the basic unit of structure and function of all living things. **9.** Schleiden and Schwann's discoveries were alike in that both stated that a specific group of living things were made up of cells. They differed in terms of the group of organisms they studied: Schleiden studied plants; Schwann studied animals. **10.** The cell theory states the following: All living things are made up of cells; cells are the basic units of structure and function in living things; all cells come from other cells. **11.** The idea about cells that proved to be false was that the material inside cells was a single substance, and that this material, called protoplasm, was the same in all cells. **12.** Suggested answer: the study of living cells would be more useful because it would yield information about the life processes of a cell.

Lesson 2 Structure of a Cell

1. The nucleus is the command center of the cell. It controls most of the activities that occur within the cell. **2.** The three parts that make up most cells are the cell membrane, the nucleus, and the cytoplasm. **3.** Cytoplasm is the living material of a cell that lies between the cell membrane and the nucleus. **4.** Lipids and proteins form the cell membrane. **5.** DNA is found in the cell's nucleus. **6.** Chromosomes are made up of proteins and nucleic acids. **7.** Nucleic acids are made up of chains of nucleotides. **8.** cytoplasm **9.** nucleus **10.** cell membrane **11.** Organelles differ among various types of cells. **12.** The cell membrane helps a cell stay balanced by controlling the flow of substances into and out of the cell, by protecting the cell from its surroundings, and by supporting and giving shape to the cell. **13.** You'd observe the nucleus of a cell because chromosomes are located within the nucleus. **14.** Suggested answer: If materials could not pass out of a cell, the cell wouldn't be able to rid itself of waste materials and would die.

Lesson 3 Cell Organelles

1. The endoplasmic reticulum is a network of passageways through which materials flow within a cell. **2.** Ribosomes produce proteins needed by the cell to carry out life processes. **3.** Mitochondria break down carbohydrates and change their energy into energy-rich molecules that the cell can use. **4.** Ribosomes are protein factories that are attached to the endoplasmic reticulum. **5.** Vacuoles are organelles in which the cell stores materials. **6.** endoplasmic reticulum **7.** mitochondrion **8.** vacuole **9.** ribosome **10.** Organelles are structures located within the cytoplasm that perform specific tasks. **11.** Much like powerhouses supply energy, mitochondria supply the cell with the energy needed to carry out life processes. **12.** Vacuoles help a cell survive by storing substances for future use or by storing wastes until they can be eliminated from the cell. **13.** If the endoplasmic reticulum of a cell is damaged, materials cannot flow throughout the cell. The other organelles would not obtain the substances they need to work. As a result, the cell wouldn't be able to carry out its life processes and would die.

14. The more active a cell, the greater the amount of energy it would need to survive. Therefore, active cells, such as muscle cells, would contain larger numbers of mitochondria than less active cells.

Lesson 4 Types of Cells

1. Chloroplasts trap the light energy necessary for photosynthesis.   **2.** Animals have specialized nerve cells and muscle cells.   **3.** The cell wall protects the plant cell and gives it support.   **4.** Specialized cells in humans make sperm and eggs for reproduction.   **5.** A eukaryotic cell contains a nucleus; a prokaryotic cell lacks a nucleus. **6.** Plant cells contain a cell wall and chloroplasts, which are not found in animal cells. **7.** Chlorophyll contained in chloroplasts traps light energy, which is changed into chemical energy through photosynthesis. This process provides the plant with the energy it needs to carry out other life processes.   **8.** Root cells absorb nutrients in plants. In humans, special cells in the intestines absorb nutrients.   **9.** Nerve cells send messages to the brain and receive messages from the brain.   **10.** Muscle cells allow animals to move around.

Lesson 5 Passive Transport

1. Diffusion is the process by which molecules of a substance move from a place of high concentration to a place of low concentration. Osmosis is the diffusion of water across a membrane.   **2.** lipids   **3.** carrier proteins   **4.** selectively permeable   **5.** diffusion **6.** higher   **7.** lower   **8.** osmosis   **9.** passive transport   **10.** Because neither process requires energy, both are classified as forms of passive transport. **11.** Molecules are constantly moving and colliding into one another. As they collide, they spread out in all directions. This motion triggers diffusion.   **12.** Certain molecules are too large to pass through the lipids in the cell membrane. Carrier proteins transport these substances across the cell membrane.   **13.** Greater amounts of the substance lie inside the cell than outside it.

Lesson 6 Cell Energy Transport and Use

1. Active transport is the process in which energy is used to transport materials across a cell membrane.   **2.** Fermentation is the process in which glucose is broken down in the absence of oxygen.   **3.** The waste products of fermentation are carbon dioxide and lactic acid. The waste products of cellular respiration are water and carbon dioxide. **4.** Cells obtain the energy necessary for active transport through cellular respiration. **5.** Both cellular respiration and fermentation break down glucose to release energy in a form the cell can use   **6.** active transport   **7.** energy   **8.** sac   **9.** cytoplasm   **10.** cellular respiration   **11.** ATP   **12.** fermentation   **13.** fermentation   **14.** cellular respiration **15.** Energy is needed when materials must be moved from an area of lower concentration to an area of greater concentration.   **16.** One form of active transport uses energy to change the shape of the cell membrane and carry molecules through it. This form is similar to the use of carrier proteins which carry substances across the cell membrane.   However, carrier proteins always move substances from areas of high concentration to areas of low concentration.   **17.** Waste materials are stored in a vacuole. The sac of wastes attaches to the cell membrane, which ruptures and expels the wastes from the cell.   **18.** Even though organisms obtain food in different ways, all organisms need to break down the food to obtain energy. Cellular respiration enables organisms to receive energy in a usable form. The cells then use this energy to carry out life processes.   **19.** Answers may include: both cellular respiration and fermentation break down glucose in food. Both processes produce ATP molecules. Both processes give off carbon dioxide as one of their waste products. However, cellular respiration occurs in the presence of oxygen, while fermentation occurs without oxygen. Mitochondria are the site of cellular respiration; fermentation occurs in the cytoplasm. Cellular respiration produces more molecules of ATP than does fermentation. Also, water is a waste product of cellular respiration, while lactic acid is a waste product of fermentation.

Lesson 7 Photosynthesis

1. Water splits into hydrogen and oxygen during the first stage, known as the light reactions.   **2.** Producers make their own food through the process of photosynthesis. **3.** Chloroplasts contain the pigment chlorophyll.   **4.** producers   **5.** photosynthesis **6.** chloroplasts   **7.** light reactions   **8.** chlorophyll   **9.** water   **10.** oxygen   **11.** dark reactions   **12.** Glucose   **13.** Chlorophyll traps energy from the sun. This provides the energy necessary for photosynthesis.   **14.** Plants need water, carbon dioxide, and sunlight for photosynthesis.   **15.** During the light stages, chlorophyll absorbs energy from the sun. This energy is used to divide water molecules into hydrogen and oxygen. **16.** During the dark stages, hydrogen combines with carbon dioxide to form glucose. **17.** The plant obtains carbon dioxide from the air   **18.** No; animal cells lack the chloroplasts and chlorophyll necessary for photosynthesis and therefore, cannot carry out this process.

Lesson 8 DNA and Cell Division

1. Spindle fibers pull chromosome pairs apart and move single chromosomes to either end of the cell.   **2.** During interphase, the parent cell makes copies of its chromosomes. **3.** Mitosis is the stage of the cell cycle during which chromosomes are distributed to two daughter cells.   **4.(a)** anaphase **(b)** prophase   **(c)** telophase **(d)** metaphase; the correct order is b, d, a, c   **5.** The cell cycle is a continuous cycle in which the cell grows, prepares for division, and divides to form two daughter cells.   **6.** Cells need to divide when they reach their size limit or can no longer transport materials throughout their structure.   **7.** Hereditary information is carried on DNA molecules in chromosomes. When a cell divides, it passes on copies of its DNA to its offspring through mitosis **8.** The four stages of mitosis are prophase, metaphase, anaphase, and telophase. **9.** Interphase is the stage of the cell cycle during which the cell copies its chromosomes. **10.** After interphase, the parent cell will contain 16 chromosomes because the cell makes copies of its chromosomes during interphase.

UNIT 1 PRACTICE TEST

1. i **2.** e **3.** f **4.** c **5.** g **6.** h **7.** j **8.** a **9.** b **10.** d   **11.** Because the diagram shows a cell wall and chloroplasts, the cell is a plant cell.   **12.** Because the diagram shows a nucleus, the cell is a eukaryotic cell.   **13.** Plant cells produce glucose through photosynthesis. During photosynthesis, a plant uses energy from the sun, carbon dioxide, and water to produce glucose and oxygen. During cellular respiration, glucose is broken down.   Glucose gives the plant the energy it needs to perform its life processes. **14.** A plant cell could obtain water from its environment through osmosis, a form of passive transport.   **15.** In both organelles, energy is changed in form.   **16.** Sketches or essays should indicate that the parent cell makes copies of its chromosomes during interphase. During mitosis, these chromosome pairs split and move to opposite ends of the cell.

Therefore, the two cells formed by the pinching of the cell membrane each contain the same number of chromosomes as the parent cell.   **17.** Drawings and essays should explain that active transport is needed to move substances from areas of lower concentration to areas of higher concentration.

Unit 2

Lesson 9 The Chemistry of Genes

1. A base triplet is a group of three bases along a strand of DNA   **2.** A gene is a portion of DNA that contains the information needed to make a specific protein   **3.** CAU **4.** mRNA brings the code from the DNA to the ribosome. tRNA connects the amino acid with the mRNA and the ribosome   **5.** Proteins are built from amino acids **6.** Ribosomes are located in a cell's protoplasm   **7.** Genes are segments of DNA **8.** The genetic code is carried in the sequence and kinds of base triplets.   **9.** C **10.** A   **11.** U   **12.** C   **13.** G   **14.** U   **15.** U   **16.** C   **17.** G   **18.** G   **19.** U   **20.** G **21.** C   **22.** DNA   **23.** mRNA   **24.** tRNA   **25.** tRNA   **26.** mRNA   **27.** protein **28.** 4, 3, 1, 6, 5, 2   **29.** The number of amino acids allows for an enormous number of different combinations of amino acid chains to be built. This, in turn, allows for the production of numerous different proteins. The traits of an organism are determined by its proteins. So, many different organisms can be created from the immense number of protein combinations.   **30.** Even within species, different genetic codes allow for differences in some proteins, resulting in variety within species.   **31.** They would be able to identify some of the proteins that existed in the body of the dinosaur. Since they only have part of the DNA, they would not know all of the proteins nor would they be able to determine what genes controlled what traits.   **32.** They would need to know which triplet was missing and from what location along the gene it was missing. They could find out this information by studying the triplet sequences in a properly coded gene from another animal of the same kind.

Lesson 10 Sex Cells and Meiosis

1. Gametes contain only one set of the chromosomes found in body cells, and thus contain half as many chromosomes.   **2.** Egg cells and sperm cells are both gametes, or sex cells. An egg cell is a female gamete, while a sperm cell is a male gamete. **3.** Through meiosis, a diploid parent cell produces haploid daughter cells.   **4.** diploid number   **5.** haploid number   **6.** gamete   **7.** meiosis   **8.** divisions   **9.** two **10.** four   **11.** egg   **12.** polar bodies   **13.** 8   **14.** 4   **15.** 16   **16.** 8   **17.** 4 **18.** A body cell contains two sets of chromosomes, resulting in a diploid number. A sex cell contains only one set of chromosomes, resulting in a haploid number.   **19.** 12 chromosomes; a gamete contains half the number of chromosomes of a body cell. **20.** During the final phase of meiosis, the female sex cell does not divide evenly. One cell receives more cytoplasm than the other three cells. This cell becomes an egg while the other, smaller cells are polar bodies. The male sex cell divides evenly during the final phase of meiosis, producing four sperm cells.   **21.** Both processes involve cell replication and division.   **22.** Mitosis begins with a diploid cell and ends with two diploid daughter cells. Meiosis begins with a diploid cell and ends with four haploid cells. This is caused by a second cell division that occurs without duplication of the chromosomes.

Lesson 11 Traits, Heredity, and Gene Expression

1. Both heterozygous and homozygous organisms have two genes for a particular trait. A homozygous organism has two genes that are alike for a particular trait while a heterozygous organism has two different genes for a particular trait.   **2.** Heredity is the passing of traits from parent to offspring.   **3.** A dominant gene hides, or masks, the recessive gene. **4.** Possible combinations are BB, bb, and Bb.   **5.** Punnett square   **6.** dominant **7.** recessive   **8.** homozygous   **9.** heterozygous   **10.** Through meiosis and sexual reproduction, offspring inherit genetic information from their parents.   **11.** A dominant gene, in this case the one for the yellow color trait, can mask a recessive gene. If both parent plants are heterozygous for the yellow/green color, their offspring could be homozygous for the green pea trait.   **12.** If a female gamete joins with a male gamete containing an X chromosome, the offspring will be female. If a female gamete joins with a male gamete containing a Y chromosome, the offspring will be male.   **13.** Yes. The person with curly hair is homozygous dominant for the trait while the person with straight hair is homozygous recessive for the trait.

Lesson 12 Mutations

1. Both are permanent changes. A gene mutation is a permanent change in the DNA of a gene. A chromosome mutation is a permanent change in the number or structure of a chromosome.   **2.** A sex-linked mutation is a permanent change in the DNA of a gene carried on either an X or a Y chromosome. **3.** DNA   **4.** gene   **5.** gene mutation **6.** sickle cell anemia   **7.** cell division   **8.** chromosome mutation   **9.** Down syndrome **10.** A gene mutation is a permanent change in the DNA of a gene. One possible cause is an error that occurs during replication which changes the DNA structure of a gene. **11.** A chromosome mutation is a permanent change in the number or structure of chromosomes in a cell. One possible cause is an error during cell division which results in the parent cell dividing unevenly. Another cause is an error which occurs when a chromosome copies itself. The chromosomes in the resulting daughter cells are different from those of the parent cell.   **12.** Mutations create variations among members of a species. It is possible that such variations enable the species to be better adapted to its environment.   **13.** A carrier for sickle cell anemia does not show the trait because of the presence of one normal gene.   **14.** Both types of mutations occur as a result of a permanent change in the DNA of a gene. A sex-linked mutation is a type of gene mutation that is carried on either an X or a Y chromosome.   **15.** Because a male gamete contains only one X chromosome, the organism needs to inherit only one X chromosome with the color blindness gene to be color blind. On the other hand, a female must inherit two X chromosomes with the color blindness genes to be colorblind.

UNIT 2 PRACTICE TEST

1. c   **2.** f   **3.** b   **4.** e   **5.** d   **6.** a   **7.** ribosomes   **8.** meiosis   **9.** protein   **10.** sex-linked mutation   **11.** DNA contains base T. RNA contains base U.   **12.** Diploid number refers to the number of chromosomes found in the body cells of an organism. Haploid number is half this amount, or the amount of chromosomes found in a gamete.   **13.** A carrier has one normal gene and one sickle cell gene and therefore does not show the disorder, since the sickle cell trait is recessive.   **14.** Color blindness is a sex-linked mutation carried on the X chromosome. For a female to be colorblind, she would have to inherit two X chromosomes carrying this mutation. A male, however, needs only to inherit one X chromosome carrying this mutation to have the disorder. Check students' Punnett squares for logic and accuracy.

15. Through meiosis, gametes are formed. These sex cells contain half the number of chromosomes found in the parent cell. By halving the number of chromosomes, meiosis ensures that gametes joined through sexual reproduction will form a diploid cell with an appropriate number of chromosomes.

Unit 3

Lesson 13 Natural Selection

1. Adaptation is the process by which an organism becomes better suited to a change in its environment. **2.** Natural selection is the term used to describe the process in which individuals best suited to their environment survive longer and reproduce more than those individuals that are not suited to their environments. **3.** As the environment changes over time, living things with helpful traits adapt to these changes. **4.** Natural selection is the process by which the species best adapted to its environment survives and reproduces. **5.** Survival of the fittest is another term for natural selection, a process in which the species best adapted to the environment survive and reproduce. **6.** moves away **7.** adapts **8.** young **9.** survival of the fittest **10.** adapted **11.** natural selection (or survival of the fittest) **12.** Different traits will allow at least some of the members to survive when and if the environment changes. **13.** Darwin's finches adapted to the different environments by having different-shaped beaks, which allowed them to eat different kinds of foods. **14.** No; only those traits that change to allow a species to survive in a new environment are the result of adaptation.

Lesson 14 Evolution of Species

1. Evolution is the process by which living things change over time. **2.** complex cells **3.** bacteria **4.** plants **5.** As environments change, those organisms with the favorable traits will survive and pass their favorable traits to their offspring. **6.** Living things were able to make their own food and gave off oxygen into the atmosphere. **7.** Over time, a species can undergo enough changes that it evolves into a new and separate species.

Lesson 15 Evidence of Evolution

1. A fossil is the preserved remains or traces of a once living thing. **2.** An ancestor is a species of the past, from which other living species have evolved. A descendant is a living species that evolved from an ancestor. **3.** fossil **4.** shell (or bone) **5.** bone (or shell) **6.** ancestors **7.** Most often, the soft parts of an animal decay, leaving only hard parts such as shells, bones, and teeth to form fossils. **8.** By looking at the fossils of their skulls and leg bones, scientists can see that horses became larger and changed in shape over time.

Lesson 16 The Beginning of Life

1. Miller's experiment showed that when energy was added to the gases found in the earth's early atmosphere-ammonia, water vapor, hydrogen, and methane-complex organic compounds such as amino acids could be formed. **2.** The early earth was covered with warm water. Violent thunderstorms and lightning were common. Ammonia, water vapor, hydrogen, and methane were found in the atmosphere. These substances dissolved in the oceans. **3.** Miller used water and the gases (water vapor, hydrogen, ammonia, and methane), heat, and extra energy. The gases simulated those that made up the atmosphere of the early earth. Heated water simulated the ancient ocean. Electricity simulated lightning. **4.** Life might have begun from the mixture of chemicals present in the atmosphere of the early earth. Adding energy to the mixture could have caused the chemicals to join together, forming complex molecules. **5.** The complex compounds could have joined together and functioned as simple cells. **6.** Humans would not be able to survive. Gases needed for respiration were not present in the early earth's atmosphere and it would have been too hot. Students may also correctly assume that there would have been too much UV radiation and nothing suitable for humans to eat.

UNIT 3 PRACTICE TEST

1. f **2.** a **3.** g **4.** c **5.** b **6.** e **7.** d **8.** adaptations **9.** survival of the fittest **10.** simple **11.** species **12.** hard **13.** similar **14.** Answers should include that there are many different traits in a population. When a change in the environment occurs, individuals with certain traits or adaptations survive, while others die. This results in a change in the traits of the population. **15.** Answers should include that conditions on the earth were very different from those of today (different gases in the atmosphere, frequent electrical storms, and a higher air temperature). Such conditions may have caused the formation of the compounds that make up living things.

Unit 4

Lesson 17 Viruses

1. A virus is a noncellular organism that is made up of genetic material and protein. **2.** A virus does not have a nucleus. **3.** Viruses can reproduce only when inside a living cell. **4.** 2, 5, 1, 3, 4 **5.** Drawings should resemble Fig. 17-2. **6.** cells **7.** reproduce or make copies of itself **8.** The two main parts of a virus are a nucleic acid and an outer protein coat. **9.** Except for reproduction, viruses lack most of the traits of cellular organisms. For example, viruses do not have a cell structure and lack a cell membrane and a nucleus. **10.** Like living things, viruses contain nucleic acids and proteins and can reproduce. **11.** They cause disease. **12.** Answers will vary but may include the idea that although viruses have some traits of nonliving things, they are closely related to living things and also impact the lives of living things.

Lesson 18 Bacteria

1. Bacteria are single-celled organisms that have no nucleus. **2.** The three shapes of bacteria are ball, rod, and spiral. **3.** Unlike most bacteria that must take in food, blue-green bacteria produce their own food by photosynthesis. **4.** Bacteria are single-celled organisms that do not have a nucleus,the cell structure that controls most cells. **5.** The cell membrane of a bacterial cell is surrounded by a cell wall that gives the bacterium its shape. The cell wall is surrounded by a thick, jelly-like capsule that protects the bacterium. **6.** Blue-green bacteria, like plants, make their own food through photosynthesis. **7.** flagella **8.** DNA **9.** cytoplasm **10.** cell membrane **11.** cell wall **12.** capsule **13.** Drawings should resemble those shown in Fig. 18-2. **14.** A bacterial cell does not have a nucleus. **15.** Bacteria are classified by shape and by the ways they get energy. **16.** Possible answers: Bacteria get energy through photosynthesis; through a host organism; or by breaking down other matter, such as dead organisms.

17. Answers will vary but may include the ideas that because there are many different types of bacteria, they can live in many different environments. Some students may reason that because bacteria are so small, there is more space for them than there is for other organisms.

Lesson 19 The Importance of Viruses and Bacteria

1. A decomposer is a living thing that breaks down dead organisms into materials that can be used by other living things.   **2.** They take in nitrogen from the air and change it into a form of nitrogen that plants can use.   **3.** An antibiotic is a drug used to treat diseases caused by bacteria   **4.** decomposers   **5.** plants   **6.** disease   **7.** antibiotics   **8.** vaccine   **9.** Answers may include: bacteria help digest food; some foods are made using bacteria; bacteria break down dead organisms; bacteria change nitrogen into a form that can be used by plants   **10.** Decomposers break down dead organisms into simpler forms that can be reused by other organisms.   **11.** Nitrogen-fixing bacteria take nitrogen from the air and form nitrogen compounds that plants can use.   **12.** A vaccine helps the body protect itself from diseases caused by viruses.   **13.** Antibiotics stop the growth of bacteria; they cannot kill viruses.   **14.** Viruses cause disease when the nucleic acid of a virus enters a cell and takes control of the cell. They also cause disease when they reproduce new copies inside a cell and cause the cell to burst.

Lesson 20 Protists

1. A chloroplast is the structure in which a plant or protist cell uses light energy and matter to make food.   **2.** The eye spot senses an area with light. The flagellum helps the euglena move to the lighted area.   **3.** A protist is a single-celled living thing that is more complex than a bacterium.   **4.** A chloroplast is the structure in which a plant or protist cell uses light energy and matter to make food.   **5.** Both cilia and flagella are used for movement. A flagellum is long and whip-like and a cilium is hair-like.   **6.** All are protists. The paramecium and amoeba are animal-like and the euglena is plantlike.   **7.** flagellum   **8.** chloroplast   **9.** nucleus   **10.** Answers will vary but should include the idea that the cell of a protist is more complex than that of a bacterium and that a protist cell has a nucleus, while a bacterial cell lacks a nucleus.   **11.** Unlike an animal-like protist, a plantlike protist has chloroplasts and can therefore make its own food.   **12.** A euglena is a plantlike protist because it can make food. It is an animal-like protist because it has a sense organ, can move from place to place, and has no cell walls.   **13.** Unlike a euglena, paramecium uses cilia instead of a flagellum for movement; paramecium has no chloroplasts.

Lesson 21 Fungi

1. Fungi are no longer classified as plants because unlike plants, fungi cannot make their own food.   **2.** Some examples of helpful fungi are decomposers, food, penicillin, and yeasts.   **3.** Fungi are living things that absorb food from living or dead things.   **4.** Hyphae are branching tubes that often grow in a tangled mass and make up the main part of a fungus.   **5.** A fruiting body is the part of a fungus that is used in reproduction.   **6.** Drawings will most likely show hyphae and a fruiting body.   **7.** Like plants, fungi have cells with cell walls and sometimes grow in soil. Fungi, however, cannot make their own food.   **8.** They both must take in and digest food.   **9.** Answers may include descriptions of bread mold, athlete's foot, Dutch elm disease, and so forth.   **10.** Yeasts give off carbon dioxide gas as they process sugar. This causes dough to rise. Bread would be very different without the action of yeasts. Some students might also indicate that yeasts are sometimes the causes of infections in people.   **11.** Mushrooms are decomposers. If no mushrooms lived in the forest, dead leaves, branches, and animals would accumulate on the forest floor. Many small plants would be covered by the debris and would not be able to grow. Without many plants, animals would have less food to eat.

UNIT 4 PRACTICE TEST

1. c **2.** i **3.** k **4.** e **5.** h **6.** d **7.** j **8.** f **9.** l **10.** g **11.** a **12.** m **13.** b
14. reproduce **15.** complex **16.** plants, animals, and protists **17.** Decomposers are important because they break down the remains of dead organisms into materials that can be reused by other living things. Bacteria and fungi are two kinds of decomposers.
18. Labels on drawings should include the nucleus, food vacuole, oral groove, mouth, cilia, and anal pore. Check drawings for logic and accuracy.

Unit 5

Lesson 22 Ferns and Mosses

1. Mosses live in moist, damp areas because they lack roots to carry water and materials into the plant and a vascular system to transport materials throughout the plant. Mosses need a constant supply of water to reproduce, so they grow in damp areas. **2.** Unlike mosses, ferns have vascular systems, true roots, and true leaves. **3.** Mosses live in damp environments where they have a constant supply of water. **4.** A fern is a higher plant that has a vascular system that transports water and nutrients throughout the plant.
5. A vascular system is a system of tubes that transports water and nutrients throughout a plant. **6.** Spores are special cells that plants, such as mosses and ferns, use for reproduction. **7.** b, d, a, c **8.** Drawings should show a fern plant with spores indicted as dark spots on the undersides of the leaves. **9.** Answers may include that both mosses and ferns reproduce with spores, both are plants, and both carry out photosynthesis.
10. Mosses do not have vascular tissue. As a result they cannot grow taller since their cells cannot easily and quickly move materials throughout the plant. **11.** Mosses cannot get water from deep in the ground and as a result usually live in moist areas.
12. Ferns have vascular tissue. Mosses do not. **13.** Answers will vary, but will generally describe asexual reproduction with spores. Spores spill out and are carried by the wind to a suitable location. When a spore lands, it grows into a new plant that releases male and female sex cells. The sex cells form a new plant that in turn releases spores and begins the cycle again. **14.** Answers will vary. Students may suggest that the climate has changed and is no longer as warm as in the past. Answers may also suggest that other plants adapted more successfully and therefore replaced ferns in many areas.

Lesson 23 Structure and Function of Higher Plants

1. The three main parts of a complex plant are the roots, leaves, and stem. **2.** Phloem carries food from the leaves to all parts of the plant. Xylem carries water and nutrients up from the roots to the stem and leaves. **3.** Tree rings form from the built-up layers of dead cell walls of xylem tissue. **4.** Plants take in carbon dioxide, water, and energy. They make food (sugar) and oxygen. **5.** Flowering plants reproduce by seeds. Sperm cells in pollen join with egg cells in the ovary to form a seed that eventually grows into a new plant. **6.** c, f, d, i, h, a, g, b, e **7.** Xylem and phloem are types of vascular tissue. Phloem carries food made in the leaves to other parts of the plant; xylem carries water and nutrients up from the roots. **8.** Photosynthesis is the process by which a plant makes food from water, carbon dioxide, and sunlight. Respiration is the opposite process, in which food is broken down and energy is released. **9.** Stomata are tiny pores in the underside of a leaf that control the amount of water that exits the leaf.
10. Male sex cells, or sperm, are found in pollen. Female sex cells, or eggs, are formed in

the ovary.   **11.** A flower matures into a fruit that protects the seeds.   **12.** Roots, leaves, and stem; roots anchor the plant in the soil and bring in water and other materials. Leaves make food.   The stem holds up leaves to light and connects the roots and leaves. **13.** When the guard cells are filled with water, they swell and cause the stomata to open. When they lose water, they get limp and the stomata close.   **14.** Answers will vary, but may include the idea that under normal conditions, the plant might lose too much water and die.

Lesson 24 Gymnosperms and Angiosperms

1. A tiny new plant and its food are inside a seed.   **2.** Seeds are the best adaptation for plant reproduction because they provide everything the young plant needs: food and protection.   **3.** Angiosperms are better adapted to reproduce than gymnosperms because their seeds are protected inside a fruit.   **4.** Gymnosperms are cone-bearing seed plants. Angiosperms are flowering seed plants. **5.** Conifers produce seeds in cones. **6.** Cones are formed by gymnosperms and do not provide much protection to seeds from the environment; flowers are produced by angiosperms and help protect seeds from the environment.   **7.** A seed contains a young plant and its food wrapped in a hard coat. It is the best adaptation for plant reproduction because the seed provides food for the young plant and protects it from damage and from drying out.   **8.** The seed is not enclosed in a flower or fruit.   **9.** Conifers are well adapted for cold or dry areas because their needle-shaped leaves are protected from drying out.   **10.** Angiosperms have a higher reproduction and survival rate because flowers and fruits protect seeds better than cones.

UNIT 5 PRACTICE TEST

1. h   **2.** c   **3.** e   **4.** a   **5.** I   **6.** b   **7.** f   **8.** d   **9.** l   **10.** g   **11.** j   **12.** k **13.** Ferns have a vascular system, true roots, and true leaves. Both ferns and mosses reproduce by spores.   **14.** Angiosperms have flowers; most gymnosperms have cones. **15.** Flowering plants are better adapted to reproduce than gymnosperms because they reproduce by covered seeds. The hard outer coat protects the seed from damage and drying out.   The traits that make flowering plants so successful are the flower and fruit that protect the seed until it is ready to germinate.   **16.** Photosynthesis is the process by which plants make food from water, carbon dioxide, and sunlight.   Respiration is the opposite process, in which food is broken down and energy released.

Unit 6

Lesson 25 Sponges and Cnidarians

1. A sponge has a body made up of two layers of cells with a jelly-like layer in between. It has a large opening at the top and a central cavity.   **2.** Asexual reproduction is a kind of reproduction that requires only one parent to produce offspring.   **3.** Sponges are filter feeders. Water carrying tiny food particles flows through the sponge and the particles are filtered out by flagella in the cells that surround the central cavity.   **4.** Sponges and cnidarians are invertebrates that live in the water, have large central cavities, and reproduce both sexually and asexually.   **5.** Tentacles are long, flexible appendages that contain stinging cells and surround the mouth of the cnidarian.   **6.** Student drawings should show water entering through the pores of the sponge moving into the central cavity and then exiting through the opening at the top of the sponge.   **7.** Sponges reproduce asexually by budding-the process in which a small bud grows on an adult, breaks off, and forms a new sponge, and by fragmentation-the process in which a piece of a sponge breaks off and eventually grows into a new sponge.   **8.** Cnidarians feed by grabbing prey with their tentacles, stinging and paralyzing the prey with stinging cells, and partially digesting food in the body cavity.   **9.** Answers will vary but may include the idea that wide-spread use of natural sponges could lead to extinction of some species.

Lesson 26 Worms

1. Flatworms have a digestive cavity with only one opening. They also have flat bodies with distinct heads and tails. Roundworms have a digestive cavity, or tube, with openings at both ends. They have smooth, tube-shaped bodies that are pointed at both ends.   **2.** A flatworm reproduces asexually by fission-the process in which an organism splits into two. It then regenerates its missing parts.   **3.** Flatworms and roundworms are two of the three kinds of worms; both have simple body forms.   **4.** Segmented worms have a tube-within-a-tube body plan. **5.** flat   **6.** simple   **7.** head (or tail) **8.** tail (or head) **9.** parasites **10.** fission **11.** pointed   **12.** most   **13.** intestines   **14.** complex **15.** segments   **16.** earthworm   **17.** eggs (or sperm)   **18.** sperm (or eggs) **19.** Adult flatworms and segmented worms produce both eggs and sperm in the same body.   **20.** The earthworm takes in soil through its mouth. As the soil passes through the body of the worm, food is removed from the soil. The soil then passes out of the worm through the anus.

Lesson 27 Mollusks

1. The four parts of a mollusk are the head, foot, mantle, and visceral mass   **2.** Univalves have a single coiled shell, a distinct head, and a large flat foot. Bivalves have two shells hinged together, no distinct head, and a wedge-shaped foot.   **3.** Bivalves are mollusks with two shells hinged together.   **4.** Univalves are mollusks that usually have one coiled shell; some univalves have no shell.   **5.** Cephalopods are mollusks that have either no shell or a small shell inside the body.   **6.** bivalves   **7.** univalve   **8.** tentacles **9.** cephalopods   **10.** bivalve   **11.** univalve   **12.** cephalopod   **13.** A bivalve has two hinged shells, a wedge-shaped foot, and no head. A univalve usually has a single coiled shell, a large flat foot, and a distinct head. A cephalopod has a small internal shell or no shell, a large head and brain, and a foot that is divided into long arms.   **14.** The structure of a slug's body is like that of other univalves; it has a distinct head with two sets of tentacles and a large flat foot that ripples as the animal moves.

Lesson 28 Arthropod Characteristics

1. An arthropod is an animal with a segmented body, a hard outer covering, and jointed legs.   **2.** An exoskeleton provides support for soft inner parts, protects the animal from drying out, and protects the animal from injury.   **3.** An arthropod is a type of complex invertebrate that has a segmented body.   **4.** An exoskeleton is a hard outer covering that provides protection to an arthropod.   **5.** Because an exoskeleton does not grow, it has to be shed or molted so the arthropod can grow a new, larger skeleton.   **6.** head (thorax or abdomen)   **7.** thorax (head or abdomen)   **8.** abdomen (head or thorax)   **9.** molts **10.** protection   **11.** antenna   **12.** claw   **13.** eye   **14.** walking legs   **15.** abdomen **16.** fused head and thorax   **17.** There are many different species of arthropods. They evolved as they adapted to each environment.   **18.** An exoskeleton does not grow and it is heavy.   **19.** Answers will vary but may include the following. If they do not compete with each other, many different species of arthropods could live in the same area and many species could evolve.

Lesson 29 Insects

1. An insect is an arthropod with three pairs of jointed legs.   **2.** Answers will vary, but should include three of the following: three pairs of jointed legs, compound and simple eyes, wings and the ability to fly, small size, and antennae.   **3.** An insect is an arthropod with three pairs of jointed legs.   **4.** Compound eyes are made up of many tiny lenses. **5.** Simple eyes cannot form images; they sense only variations in light.   **6.** three **7.** small   **8.** antennae   **9.** fly   **10.** hundreds of   **11.** Answers will vary but may include that bees pollinate food crops and butterflies pollinate flowers.   **12.** Answers will vary but may include the following: insects are generally small and need little space or food. There are many different species with different needs, so many species do not compete with each other. They have well-developed senses with which to find food and escape danger. They can fly to find new sources of food and new places to live and to escape danger. They reproduce in large numbers.

Lesson 30 Other Arthropods

1. Answers should include three of the following differences: arachnids have four pairs of legs, no wings, two body regions, and no antennae.   **2.** Arachnids are arthropods with four pairs of jointed legs.   **3.** Crustaceans are arthropods with five pairs of jointed legs. **4.** Centipedes are arthropods with one pair of jointed legs attached to most of their body segments.   **5.** Millipedes are arthropods with two pairs of jointed legs attached to most of their body segments.   **6.** crustaceans   **7.** five   **8.** two   **9.** arachnid **10.** four   **11.** two   **12.** millipedes (or centipedes)   **13.** centipedes (or millipedes) **14.** one   **15.** two   **16.** Spiders catch their prey by hunting or trapping. Then a spider injects the prey with poison, which paralyzes the prey.   **17.** Centipedes have one pair of legs on most of their body segments, while millipedes have two pairs of legs on most of their body segments.

Lesson 31 Echinoderms

1. An adult echinoderm has radial symmetry instead of left-right symmetry.   **2.** Tube feet are water-filled suction cups that are used by starfish for movement and feeding. **3.** *Echinoderm* means "spiny-skinned."   **4.** Radial symmetry is a body plan in which body parts repeat around an imaginary line drawn through a central area.   **5.** Tube feet are used by echinoderms to get food, such as by aiding in opening clam shells.   **6.** ocean **7.** internal   **8.** feeding, movement (in any order)   **9.** In left-right symmetry division along only one axis will result in mirror images; in radial symmetry, there are several axes along which division will result in mirror images.   **10.** Cutting up the starfish would cause them to regenerate resulting in more starfish. This would likely result in a decrease in the clam population.

UNIT 6 PRACTICE TEST

1. invertebrates   **2.** sponges   **3.** budding, fragmentation (in any order)   **4.** Cnidarians **5.** flatworms   **6.** parasites   **7.** segmented worms   **8.** earthworm   **9.** arthropods **10.** exoskeleton   **11.** Insects   **12.** compound eye   **13.** arachnid   **14.** Crustaceans **15.** Centipedes   **16.** Echinoderms   **17.** Echinoderms have radial symmetry; most other animals have left-right symmetry.   **18.** Flatworms have flat bodies and are the simplest worms. Roundworms have long, thin bodies that are pointed at both ends. Segmented have segmented bodies and are the most complex type of worm.   **19.** An animal is successful if it can survive and reproduce in its environment and if it can adapt to changes in the environment. Insects are successful because of their small size, the fact that they can live in almost any type of environment, eat anything, and that they reproduce quickly and in large numbers.   **20.** Student answers will vary, but should include the basic characteristics of arthropods: jointed legs, exoskeleton, and segmented body. Students can show their imagination in describing how the animal looks and moves and how it reproduces and what it eats.

Unit 7

Lesson 32 Vertebrate Characteristics

1. The five major groups of vertebrates are: fishes, amphibians, reptiles, birds, and mammals.
2. The characteristic that distinguishes a vertebrate from other animals is the backbone.
3. Chordates are animals that at some time in their life have a nerve cord, a flexible rod that supports the body, and gill slits.   Vertebrates are one kind of chordate.
4. Vertebrates are animals that have a strong, flexible backbone made up of small bones called vertebrae. **5.** vertebrates **6.** chordates **7.** endoskeleton **8.** fishes **9.** amphibians
10. reptiles   **11.** birds   **12.** mammals   **13.** Answers should include the respiratory, circulatory, digestive, skeletal, reproductive, excretory, and nervous systems (in any order).
14. Answers will vary but should include some of the following traits of vertebrates: well-defined organ systems, head with sense organs, and endoskeleton.

Lesson 33 Fishes

1. An ectothermic animal is one whose body temperature changes with its environment.
2. Fishes are vertebrates that live in water and breathe with gills.   **3.** Jawless fishes and cartilaginous fishes are the two smallest groups of fishes. Jawless fishes have smooth, round bodies; flexible skeletons; and no jaws. Cartilaginous fishes have jaws and flexible skeletons made of cartilage.   **4.** Cartilaginous fishes have jaws and flexible skeletons made of cartilage.   **5.** eye   **6.** head   **7.** trunk   **8.** teeth   **9.** gills   **10.** fins
11. tail   **12.** Answers should include three of the following: vertebrate that lives in water, breathes with gills, is ectothermic, has three distinct body parts, fins, scales, and a two-chambered heart.   **13.** Jawless fishes are the only fishes that have no jaws.   **14.** A bony fish has a skeleton made of bone; a cartilaginous fish has a flexible skeleton made of cartilage.   **15.** Because fishes are ectothermic animals, their body temperature changes with the temperature of the water in which they live. Cool water would lower their body temperatures and they would die.

Lesson 34 Evolution of Land Vertebrates

1. Three benefits to living on land are new sources of food and places to live, 20 percent more oxygen to breathe, and more places that offer protection and shelter in which to raise offspring.   **2.** Lungs are the primary internal organs of the respiratory system of land vertebrates.   **3.** They need the strong skeleton to support their body weight.
4. External fertilization takes place outside a female's body and requires water to move sperm to the egg. Internal fertilization takes place inside a female's body and does not require water to move sperm to the egg.   **5.** Endothermic animals are able to maintain a constant internal body temperature; the temperature of ectothermic animals changes with the temperature of their environment. **6.** shelter (or food)   **7.** food (or shelter)
8. oxygen   **9.** lungs **10.** skeletons **11.** Endothermic **12.** Some land vertebrates have scales and secrete a slimy substance (mucus) to cover the skin.   **13.** Land

vertebrates have internal fertilization and many land vertebrates lay eggs with a leathery or hard outer shell.   **14.** Answers will vary, but should include that humans would have to have a new way to breathe, move, reproduce, eat, remove wastes, and so forth.

Lesson 35 Amphibians

1. Mucus glands on the skin keep the skin from drying out.   **2.** Most adult amphibians have lungs and live on land.   **3.** Tadpoles are immature frogs.   **4.** vertebrates **5.** land (or water)   **6.** water (or land)   **7.** lungs   **8.** gills   **9.** mucus glands   **10.** external   **11.** tadpoles   **12.** The two main kinds of amphibians are tailless amphibians such as toads and frogs and those with tails such as salamanders.   **13.** Answers should include three of the following: internal lungs instead of external gills, mucus glands in skin to keep it moist, strong limbs for walking, and strong bony skeletons to support body weight. **14.** Amphibians have internal lungs instead of external gills, live on land instead of water, have a three-chambered heart instead of a two-chambered heart; and have two pairs of limbs.   **15.** Tadpoles have a tail; adult frogs do not. Tadpoles breathe through gills; frogs have lungs. Tadpoles have no legs; frogs have two pairs of legs. Tadpoles are a plant-eaters; frogs eat other animals, mostly insects. Tadpoles live in the water; some frogs live on land.

Lesson 36 Reptiles

1. Three characteristics of reptiles that allow them to live on land are internal fertilization, an amniotic egg, and thick skin covered with scales.   **2.** A reptile is an invertebrate with an amniotic egg that protects the offspring from drying out during its development. **3.** A reptile is an invertebrate that reproduces by internal fertilization. Internal fertilization takes place inside the female's body and does not require water to move the sperm to the egg.   **4.** vertebrates **5.** land **6.** internal **7.** amniotic **8.** drying out **9.** four **10.** tuatara **11.** Turtles (or Tortoises) **12.** tortoises (or turtles) **13.** Crocodiles (or Alligators) **14.** alligators (or crocodiles) **15.** Lizards **16.** snakes **17.** A snake does not have legs; a lizard does.   **18.** Answers may include: a tuatara has a long tail and a scaly crest that runs down its back and neck; turtles and tortoises have bodies protected by a two-part shell; crocodiles and alligators have strong tails for swimming and strong jaws and sharp teeth for capturing prey; lizards have legs; snakes do not have legs. **19.** Amphibians and reptiles are ectothermic vertebrates, most of which have two pairs of legs, and a three-chambered heart. Unlike amphibians, reptiles have an amniotic egg, internal fertilization, and thick scales.

Lesson 37 Birds

1. Birds have feathers, wings, lightweight bones, and air sacs throughout their bodies. **2.** Feathers are modified scales adapted for flight and for conserving body heat.   **3.** A bird is an endothermic vertebrate that can fly.   **4.** Birds are vertebrates that have a body covering of feathers and special traits for flight.   **5.** feathers (or wings)   **6.** wings (or feathers)   **7.** constant   **8.** internal   **9.** amniotic   **10.** four   **11.** endothermic **12.** feathers (or air sacs)   **13.** air sacs (or feathers)   **14.** lightweight   **15.** Feathers help the bird fly and maintain its constant body temperature.   **16.** Four common groups of birds and some examples follow: water birds-ducks, geese, swans, heron, flamingo, sandpiper, gulls; birds of prey-hawks, eagles, owls; flightless birds-penguins, emus (rhea), ostriches; perching birds-robins, sparrows, and other songbirds.   **17.** Birds are different from most other vertebrates because birds have feathers and can fly.

Lesson 38 Mammals

1. A mammal is a vertebrate that has mammary glands, hair, and gives birth.   **2.** Hair protects the skin from injury and insulates the body.   **3.** A duck-billed platypus lays eggs. **4.** The placenta is a special organ that connects the unborn mammal to the mother inside the mother's body.   **5.** Mammals are vertebrates that have mammary glands that produce milk to feed to the young after it is born.   **6.** Mammals and birds both are endothermic and have four-chambered hearts. **7.** egg-laying **8.** laying eggs **9.** spiny anteater **10.** inside the mother's pouch **11.** kangaroo   **12.** placental   **13.** inside the placenta **14.** human   **15.** Mammals have hair, mammary glands, and give birth.   **16.** A well-developed brain helps a mammal adapt to its environment and direct many kinds of complex behavior.   **17.** Platypi and spiny anteaters (echidna) lay eggs. Pouched mammals give birth to undeveloped young that develop in the mother's pouch. The young of placental mammals develop in the placenta and are born fully developed.

UNIT 7 PRACTICE TEST

1. vertebrate   **2.** Fishes   **3.** jawless, cartilaginous, bony (in any order)   **4.** ectothermic **5.** reptile   **6.** amniotic   **7.** placenta   **8.** Answers will vary but should include at least three of the following: a backbone, well-developed organ systems, complex body plan, a head with sense organs.   **9.** Likely responses will include: fishes are ectothermic, live in water, and have external fertilization. Birds are endothermic, can fly, and have internal fertilization. Accept all logical responses.   **10.** Amphibians have mucus covering their skin, breathe with gills when young, and with lungs as adults, and reproduce by forming jelly-like eggs that must be kept moist. Reptiles have a thick, scaly skin, breathe with lungs, and produce eggs with thick, leathery shells that won't dry out on land.   **11.** Mammal traits that help them survive and reproduce include: complex and large brains that allow them to adapt and have complex types of behavior, a covering of hair that insulates them, internal fertilization, and the birth of well-developed offspring. Mothers provide nutrition to their young with milk from mammary glands. Parents care for the offspring until they are ready to live and survive on their own.   **12.** The charts will vary but should include whether each animal is endothermic or ectothermic, has internal or external fertilization, where it lives, the number of chambers in its heart, and its kind of skeleton.

Unit 8

Lesson 39 Ecosystems and Interactions

1. All the living parts of an ecosystem make up a community. A population is all the members of a particular species within a community.   **2.** An ecosystem is both the living and the nonliving factors that surround an organism. The living factors within an ecosystem make up a community.   **3.** In a single community, there are many populations, or groups of organisms of the same species.   **4.** Competition and predation are two relationships between organisms. **5.** ecosystem   **6.** community   **7.** populations   **8.** Predation **9.** Competition **10.** Commensalism   **11.** Mutualism **12.** An ecosystem consists of all the living and nonliving things in an area that interact with one another.   **13.** Predation is a relationship between organisms in which one organism kills and eats another. **14.** Competition is the struggle between living things to obtain the resources necessary for their survival. It occurs because resources are often limited. **15.** Commensalism and mutualism are alike in that both relationships benefit organisms. In commensalism, one organism in the partnership is helped while the other organism is unaffected. In mutualism, both partners benefit **16.** Competition occurred when the two hawks tried to get nutrition on the form of the same rabbit. Predation occurred when the hawk, the predator, caught and ate the rabbit, the prey. **17.** The drop in number of snowshoe hares would increase competition among the lynx to obtain food. The lynx population would experience a similar drop in population.

Lesson 40 Energy Flow in Ecosystems

1. A producer can make its own food, while a consumer must obtain food from an outside source. **2.** energy **3.** producers **4.** consumers **5.** Decomposers **6.** ecosystem **7.** food chain **8.** food web **9.** energy pyramid **10.** A food chain could never begin with a consumer because these organisms must ultimately obtain energy from an outside source. A food chain will always start with a producer. **11.** Decomposers break down nonliving organic material, returning nutrients back to the ecosystem. Producers need these nutrients to carry out photosynthesis. **12.** Energy is constantly lost to the ecosystem in the form of heat. As a result, the amount of energy present at the upper level of an energy pyramid is always less than that present at the lower levels. **13.** As the amount of energy decreases, the number of organisms that can be supported also decreases. Energy is lost at every level of the energy pyramid. Thus, the upper levels contain fewer organisms than the lower levels.

Lesson 41 Biomes

1. A biome is a large geographic area with a certain climate and specific types of communities. **2.** They are inactive because there is little energy available and they need to conserve it. **3.** The sublittoral zone gets a large amount of energy from the sun and a large supply of nutrients. **4.** littoral zone **5.** sublittoral zone **6.** pelagic zone **7.** The six land biomes are the tundra, taiga, deciduous forest, tropical rain forest, desert, and grassland. **8.** Populations reside in the biome for which they are physically suited and where they can find the resources they need to survive. **9.** There is a constant amount of sunlight all year. The year-round availability of energy makes the tropical rain forest biome ideal for supporting a hugely diverse number of species. **10.** All the solar energy is concentrated in the first 200 meters of the pelagic zone. The organisms below this depth cannot get energy directly from the sun, so they must eat organisms that do.

Lesson 42 Human Impact on Ecosystems

1. The wise use of natural resources, or materials in the environment used by people, is conservation. **2.** Renewable resources can be replaced, while non-renewable resources cannot. **3.** natural resources **4.** Renewable **5.** Non-renewable **6.** harmful **7.** Smog **8.** acid rain **9.** pesticides **10.** factories **11.** natural resources **12.** Conservation **13.** Recycling **14.** A renewable resource can be replaced, while a non-renewable resource cannot. **15.** As the human population has increased, the demand for resources has also increased. Greater amounts of resources are needed to maintain modern lifestyles. A by-product of these modern lifestyles is the release of harmful pollutants in the environment. **16.** Burning fuels for heat, electricity, and transportation are the main sources of air pollution. **17.** Acid rain forms when certain gases, from burning fuel, mix with water vapor in the air. The acids that form fall to the earth in rainwater.   **18.** Acid rain that falls into lake ecosystems pollutes the water, killing individual organisms, and sometimes, entire populations, of the ecosystem's communities. **19.** Conservation is the wise use of natural resources.   **20.** Humans can help preserve natural resources through conservation and recycling.

UNIT 8 PRACTICE TEST

1. c   **2.** d   **3.** f   **4.** a   **5.** h   **6.** i   **7.** b   **8.** e   **9.** g   **10.** A population is all members of a particular species of organism in an ecosystem. All the populations in the ecosystem make up a community.   **11.** Energy from the sun is taken in and used by producers to make food.   **12.** Renewable natural resources, such as trees, can be replaced by natural processes. Non-renewable resources, such as coal, cannot be replaced once they are used.   **13.** Most organisms are physically adapted to life in only a certain type of biome. Many organisms of the rain forest can survive only in their own small area of the forest. Also, most organisms are adapted to certain energy needs. Some organisms can survive in area where solar energy is limited in the winter. Many other organisms can live only where they can receive a constant amount of energy from the sun year round. **14.** People have harmed ecosystems by polluting the earth's air and water supplies. In addition, people have destroyed ecosystems through their activities such as mining and logging, and construction on environmentally sensitive land. People can help preserve the earth's ecosystems by conserving and recycling natural resources.

Unit 9

Lesson 43 Bone, Muscle, and Skin

1. Ligaments are strips of connective tissue that join bones at a joint.   **2.** Many bones form from tough, flexible tissue called cartilage.   **3.** Tendons connect skeletal muscles to bones.   **4.** The outer layer of the skin is the epidermis, and the inner layer is the dermis. **5.** muscles   **6.** bones   **7.** joints   **8.** contract   **9.** tendons   **10.** move   **11.** energy **12.** cellular respiration   **13.** The skeletal system allows movement, provides the body with shape and support, protects internal organs, makes blood cells, and stores minerals. **14.** As ligaments stretch, bones move at a joint.   **15.** Tendons connect muscles to bones. Ligaments connect one bone to another bone.   **16.** A hinge joint allows bones to move back and forth. A ball-and-socket joint allows bones to move in all directions. **17.** Involuntary muscles move without conscious thought. Cardiac muscles that make up the heart and smooth muscles that make up internal organs are involuntary muscles. Voluntary muscles are controlled by thought. Skeletal muscles are voluntary muscles. **18.** Skeletal muscles work in pairs to move bones at a joint. A signal from the brain causes one of the muscles to contract. As it contracts, it pulls on tendons. This in turn, exerts force on a bone, causing it to move. The other muscle in the pair relaxes, permitting the movement. **19.** The outer layer of skin, the epidermis, is a thin barrier that helps prevent water loss and protects the body from germs. The inner layer of skin, the dermis, contains the nerves, blood vessels, hair follicles, oil glands, and sweat glands. Waste products and water are eliminated from the body through the sweat glands.

Lesson 44 Circulatory and Respiratory Systems

1. Both are vessels through which blood flows. Arteries carry blood away from the heart while veins carry blood to the heart. The arteries have more muscle in their walls than do veins.   **2.** pump   **3.** atria   **4.** ventricles   **5.** Arteries   **6.** Veins   **7.** capillaries **8.** Red blood cells   **9.** White blood cells   **10.** Platelets   **11.** Plasma   **12.** lungs

13. alveoli   14. bronchi   15. lungs   16. alveoli   17. diaphragm   18. The right side of the heart pumps blood to the lungs while the left side of the heart pumps blood throughout the body.   19. Valves act asone-way doors between the atrium and ventricle on each side of the heart. By opening and closing at certain times, the valves prevent the backward flow of blood.   20. Arteries carry blood away from the heart. Veins carry blood back to the heart. Capillaries are very thin vessels through which substances move into and out of the blood.   21. Red blood cells carry oxygen throughout the body. White blood cells protect the body against infection.

Lesson 45 Digestion and Excretory Systems

1. mouth   2. mechanical   3. saliva   4. pharynx   5. stomach   6. small   7. pancreas   8. blood stream   9. large   10. excretory   11. kidneys   12. urine   13. urinary bladder   14. The thick, muscular esophagus contracts in wavelike motions, which causes food to move downward into the stomach.   15. Stomach muscles contract, churning food and breaking it into small pieces.   16. The liver produces an enzyme that is released through the gallbladder into the small intestine. This and other enzymes chemically digest food.   17. Digested food passes through projections in the lining of the small intestine and into the bloodstream where it is carried to body cells. 18. The main job of the kidneys is to filter the blood. To filter the blood, the kidneys reabsorb any substances needed by the body and eliminate waste products from the cells. 19. Arteries carry blood to clusters of capillaries in the kidneys. Nutrients move from the blood through the capillaries and into cuplike sacs. In a connected tube, the nutrients are passed back into capillaries where they are returned to the bloodstream and carried to body cells.   20. The throat opens into two tubes–the trachea and esophagus. When breathing, the flap closes off the esophagus. When swallowing, the flap covers the trachea. If people speak and eat at the same time, the flap may not cover the correct tube. Food could accidentally go down the trachea and cut off the person's air supply.

Lesson 46 Nervous System and Senses

1. Neurons carry messages throughout the body.   2. neurons   3. messages 4. Sense 5. brain 6. cerebrum   7. cerebellum 8. medulla   9. The nervous system receives and relays information about activities within the body; monitors and responds to internal and external changes; and receives and responds to messages about the environment. 10. Both dendrites and axons receive messages. Dendrites carry messages to the cell body while axons carry messages away from the cell body.   11. The brain is called the control center of the body because it interprets and reacts to impulses. 12. The ears detect energy in the form of sound waves.   13. Special cells in the sense organs detect energy. The cells send a message to neurons to relay the message through the spinal cord to the brain. The brain interprets the message.

Lesson 47 Reproduction and Development

1. The testes are the main organs of the male reproductive system. The ovaries are the main organs of the female reproductive system.   2. During menstruation, cells from the uterus and the unfertilized egg pass out of the female's body.   3. The umbilical cord connects the embryo to the placenta. Blood vessels in the umbilical cord carry nutrients and oxygen to the embryo.   4. Sperm are produced in the testes.   5. Eggs are produced in the ovaries.   6. Ovulation occurs at about the midway point of a female's menstrual cycle.   7. Fertilization is the joining of the sperm and the egg. The fertilized egg is called a zygote. 8. (a) testis (b) scrotum (c) urethra (d) penis   (e) ovary (f) fallopian tube   (g) uterus (h) cervix   (i) vagina 9. The reproductive system produces, stores, and releases specialized sex cells called gametes.   10. The position of

the scrotum outside the male's body causes lower temperature in the testes than in the body. This lower temperature is necessary for sperm production.   **11.** As a mature egg leaves an ovary, it moves into a fallopian tube, to the uterus, and finally passes from the female through the vagina.   **12.** During the menstrual cycle, hormones trigger a build-up, or thickening, of the walls of the uterus. If fertilization does not occur, the walls break apart. These cells then pass out of the female through menstruation.   **13.** No. For an egg and sperm to join, a mature egg must first be released by an ovary. Therefore, ovulation must occur before fertilization.   **14.** The placenta, which connects mother and child, supplies the developing embryo with nutrients and oxygen while removing carbon dioxide and wastes.   **15.** The stages of the human life cycle include infancy, childhood, adolescence, adulthood, and old age.

Lesson 48   Immune System

1. Answers should include five of the following nonspecific defenses: skin; mucus; cilia; digestive juices; body secretions such as sweat, saliva, and tears, and the inflammatory response.   **2.** AIDS is caused by HIV.   **3.** pathogens   **4.** immune system **5.** Nonspecific   **6.** skin   **7.** Specific   **8.** antigen   **9.** antibodies   **10.** Nonspecific defenses are not directed at a particular type of pathogen, but guard against all disease-causing substances. Specific defenses are unique responses of the immune system against a particular type of substance.   **11.** Body secretions such as tears contain enzymes that break down a variety of different pathogens.   **12.** The inflammatory response is a process by which special white blood cells move from the blood into tissue where pathogens lie. The blood cells surround and destroy the pathogens.   **13.** T-cells are white blood cells that directly attack the cells of pathogens by transferring proteins into the invading cell, causing it to rupture and die.   **14.** HIV destroys white blood cells that identify antigens, produce antibodies, and destroy invading antigens.   **15.** The immune system of an AIDS patient is damaged by HIV, limiting the person's ability to fight disease. As a result, the common cold can be life-threatening to an AIDS patient.

UNIT 9 PRACTICE TEST

1. f   **2.** d   **3.** h   **4.** e   **5.** a   **6.** b   **7.** c   **8.** g   **9.** Tendons connect muscles to the bones. The muscles work in pairs to move the bones. When a muscle contracts, it pulls the bone to which it is attached in the same direction the muscle is moving. At the same time, the other muscle of the pair relaxes, allowing the bone to move.   **10.** The lungs remove carbon dioxide from the blood and release it from the body. The major organs of the excretory system, the kidneys, filter the wastes from blood. **11.** Both mechanical and chemical digestion take place in the stomach. The stomach walls secrete gastric juices containing enzymes. Gastric juices chemically digest food. Contractions of the muscular stomach walls mix food with the juices, mechanically digesting the food. These processes turn food into a thick liquid. Gastric juices also break apart pathogens that enter the digestive system.   **12.** The testes are the primary reproductive organs of the male and the ovaries are the primary reproductive organs of the female. Both produce gametes.   **13.** Answers will vary but the drawings and essays should include the following information. Fertilization occurs when an egg and sperm cell join. The fertilized egg, or zygote, moves to the uterus. The cells of the zygote divide, forming a hollow ball of cells. The cell ball attaches to the uterus wall. The developing offspring is then called an embryo. Tissues in the uterus develop into the placenta.

The embryo develops inside the female's uterus for about nine months.   **14.** Answers will vary but the drawings and essays should include mention of the response by at least one of the following nonspecific defense responses. Natural openings to the body, such as the mouth and nose, contain mucus and/or hairs that trap pathogens. Cilia and mucus in the respiratory system also trap pathogens. Digestive juices in the stomach break apart pathogens that enter the digestive system. Body secretions, such as tears, saliva, and sweat, also contain enzymes that break down pathogens. The inflammatory response is one in which special white blood cells move from the blood and into the tissue containing the pathogen. The white blood cells then surround the pathogen and destroy it. Examples of specific defense responses include: The immune system sends special proteins, called antibodies, to destroy a pathogen. The antibodies form as a reaction to the presence of an antigen. The body recognizes the specific type of antigen, then produces the proper antibody. The antibodies bond with the antigens to help destroy the pathogen. Another specific defense is a special type of white blood cell, called a T-cell. T-cells directly attack the cells of pathogens. The T-cells transfer proteins directly into the cell membrane of the pathogen causing the invading cell to rupture and die.

Unit 1 TEST

Cells and the Chemistry of Life

Name:_____ Date:_____

Use the following terms below to label the parts of the cell shown in the numbered spaces provided:

cell membrane

endoplasmic reticulum

mitochondria

nucleus

ribosomes

1._____

2._____

3._____

4._____

5._____

Answer the following questions.

6. Explain the difference between a eukaryotic cell and a prokaryotic cell.

_____

_____

7. Describe the function of mitochondria.

_____

_____

8. Describe the functions of the nucleus.

_____

_____

9. What is the difference between active transport and passive transport?

_____

_____

10. Answer one of the following questions.

   a. In a chart or paragraph describe the functions of the following organelles. Tell if they appear in plant cells, animal cells, or both.

   nucleus   cell membrane   cell wall   mitochondria   cytoplasm
        chromosomes   vacuoles   chloroplasts   ribosomes

   b. To kill grass and other plants growing in sidewalk cracks, people sometimes sprinkle salt on the plants. Use what you know about osmosis to explain why sprinkling a plant with salt kills the plant.

Genetics and Heredity

Name:_____ Date:_____

Match each definition in Column B with its term in Column A.

Column A

____ 1. diploid number

____ 2. meiosis

____ 3. gene

____ 4. dominant gene

____ 5. homozygous

Column B

a. having two genes that are the same for one trait

b. portion of DNA that contains the information needed to make a specific protein

c. number of chromosomes in the body cells of an organism

d. type of cell division that produces gametes

e. gene that dominates, or masks, another gene for the same trait

Write a brief answer in the space provided.

6. Explain the difference between mRNA and tRNA.

_____

_____

7. What is the difference between a dominant gene and a recessive gene?

_____

_____

8. Explain the difference between the terms *homozygous* and *heterozygous*.

_____

_____

9. Explain how a chromosome mutation occurs.

_____

_____

10. Answer one of the following questions.

   a. The gene for bushy eyebrows is dominant. The gene for narrow eyebrows is recessive. Use a Punnett Square to predict the traits of offspring from a homozygous mother with narrow eyebrows and a heterozygous father with bushy eyebrows.

   b. Explain the chemical basis for why there are so many different types of organisms in the world

Name:_____ Date:_____

Match each definition in Column B with its term in Column A.

Column A	Column B

Column A

a. descendant

b. evolution

c. fossil

d. natural selection

e. species

f. organic compound

g. ancestor

Column B

_____ 1. process by which living things change over time

_____ 2. living species that has evolved from an ancestor

_____ 3. chemical compound that contains carbon

_____ 4. group of closely related living things that can mate with each other and produce young that can also produce young

_____ 5. preserved remains or traces of once-living things

_____ 6. process by which organisms with certain traits survive and reproduce

_____ 7. living species of the past, from which other living species have evolved

Fill in the blank spaces in the statements below.

8. To survive in a changed environment, an organism must either move away

   or _____.

9. The process by which an organism becomes better suited to a change in its

   environment is called _____.

10. Another term for natural selection is _____.

11. As a result of natural selection, groups of living things can change so much
    that they become new _____.

12. Modern scientists explain evolution by studying an organism's _____.

13. By studying fossils, scientists can see that many animals alive today have

    common _____.

14. The first living things appeared on the earth more than _____ years ago.

15. Answer one of the following questions.

    a. In your own words, explain how life might have first appeared on the earth.

    b. Explain the relationship between ancestors and descendants.

Microbes and Fungi

Name:_____ Date:_____

Use the terms listed below to fill in the blanks.

cilia	capsule	vaccine	antibiotic
virus	decomposer	nucleus	paramecium
flagellum	blue-green bacteria	reproduction	
bacteria	amoeba	nitrogen-fixing bacteria	

1. A drug that helps the body protect itself from infection by a virus is

   a(n) _____.

2. A(n) _____ breaks down once-living matter into simple materials that can be reused by other living things.

3. Very simple single-celled living things that lack a nucleus are _____.

4. _____ is the process of making more of the same kind.

5. Bacteria that take nitrogen from the air and form nitrogen compounds that can be used

   by plants are called _____.

6. A very small particle made up of a nucleic acid and a protein is a(n)

   _____.

7. The _____ is the cell structure that controls most cell activities and is not present in bacteria.

8. The layer that protects a bacterial cell and is found outside the cell wall is

   the _____.

9. Bacteria that make their own food are called _____.

10. A long, whip-like structure that helps some types of cells move from place to place is

    a(n) _____.

11. A(n) _____ is an animal-like protist that moves with cilia.

12. _____ are tiny hairs on the outside of some cells that push the cell through the water.

13. An animal-like protist that moves by changing its shape is the _____.

14. A(n) _____ is a drug used to treat diseases caused by bacteria.

15. Answer one of the following questions.

    a. Explain how bacteria can be both harmful and helpful to humans.

    b. Draw a bacteria and label its main parts.

Name:_____ Date:_____

Complete the following statements.

1. The _____ system is made up of tubes that carry water and other materials throughout a plant.

2. A(n) _____ is a type of simple plant that does not have tissue to transport water and other materials throughout its structure.

3. The part of the flower in which egg cells form is the _____.

4. The _____ is a special reproductive structure of a plant that contains a young plant and its food.

5. A(n) _____ is a type of seed plant whose seeds are usually found inside a cone, not inside a flower.

6. The most common type of seed plants are _____.

7. The process by which plants make food is called _____.

8. The_____ is a special reproductive structure in which seeds form.

9. _____ are the reproductive cells of mosses and ferns.

10. Vascular tissue that carries food made in the leaves to all other parts of the plant is called _____.

11. A(n) _____ protects one or more seeds.

12. A(n) _____ is a type of complex plant that has a vascular system and reproduces by means of spores.

Answer the following questions.

13. What is the main difference between mosses and ferns?

_____

_____

14. How are gymnosperms adapted to life in dry areas?

_____

_____

15. Answer one of the following questions.

   a. What would happen to a plant if its roots were removed? Explain your answer.

   b. Florists sometimes sell carnations that have been dyed colors such as blue and green. The dye is added to the flower's water. How do you think the dye gets to the flower?

Unit 6 TEST

Invertebrates

Name:_____ Date:_____

Complete the following statements.

1. _____ reproduction does not require fertilization to produce offspring.

2. A smooth, tube-shaped worm that is pointed at both ends is a(n) _____.

3. A(n) _____ is a mollusk that has two shells hinged together.

4. To _____ is to shed an old exoskeleton before a new one grows.

5. A_____ eye can sense only light and dark and cannot form images.

6. An arthropod with two pairs of jointed legs attached to most of its body

   segments is a(n) _____.

7. _____ are long, flexible appendages surrounding the mouth of a
   cnidarian.

8. The _____ is the fold of skin that wraps around and protects the
   visceral mass of a mollusk.

9. An invertebrate with a soft body that is usually covered by one or more

   hard shells is a(n) _____.

10. _____ symmetry is a body plan in which body parts are arranged
    in a circle around a central area.

11. A(n)_____ is a mollusk that has either no shell or a small shell
    inside its body.

12. _____ are water-filled suction cups used by starfish for movement
    and feeding.

Answer the following questions.

13. What are the differences between sponges and cnidarians?

    _____

    _____

14. What are the three main characteristics of arthropods?

    _____

    _____

15. Answer one of the following questions.

    a. Compare the feeding behaviors of flatworms, roundworms, and
       segmented worms.

    b. What do you think the earth would be like if there were no insects?

Name:_____ Date:_____

Complete the following statements.

1. A(n) _____is a vertebrate that has mammary glands, gives

   birth, and has a body covered with _____.

2. A(n) _____ is an animal that has a thin, flexible rod that

   supports three features: the body, gill slits, and a _____ cord.

3. A bird is an endothermic vertebrate that has _____ and

   _____.

4. The primary internal organs of the respiratory system of land vertebrates are the

   _____.

5. _____ glands in the skin of some vertebrates produce a

   slimy substance that keeps the skin from drying out.

6. The five main groups of vertebrates are _____, _____,

   _____, _____, and _____.

7. The _____ of vertebrates provides support and protection.

Answer the following questions.

8. What is the difference between an endothermic animal and an ectothermic animal?

   _____

   _____

9. What is the difference between internal and external fertilization?

   _____

   _____

10. Answer one of the following questions.

    a. Describe three differences between fishes and reptiles.

    b. Compare breathing and reproduction of vertebrates living in the water to
       those living on land.

Ecology

Name:_____ Date:_____

Match each definition in Column B with its term in Column A.

Column A

_____ 1. competition

_____ 2. producer

_____ 3. pollution

_____ 4. renewable resource

_____ 5. energy pyramid

_____ 6. predation

_____ 7. food chain

Column B

a. model that shows the flow of energy through organisms in an ecosystem

b. model that shows how energy is lost in a food chain

c. natural resource that can be replaced

d. any harmful substance in the environment

e. organism that can make its own food

f. relationship in which one organism kills and eats another

g. struggle between living things to obtain what they need to survive

Give a brief answer for each of the following.

8. Compare and contrast commensalism and mutualism.

_____

_____

_____

9. Explain the relationship among producers, consumers, and decomposers.

_____

_____

_____

10. Answer one of the following questions.

    a. Explain how the rain forest, deciduous forest, and taiga biomes differ.

    b. What are three ways that people can save the earth's ecosystems?

Name:_____ Date:_____

Use the words listed to complete the following sentences.

circulatory   *respiratory*   *reproductive*

skeletal   *muscular*

1. The _____ system produces offspring
2. The _____ system helps bones move the body.
3. The _____ system gives the body shape and support.
4. The _____ system moves blood throughout the body.
5. The _____ system brings oxygen into the body.

Answer each question in the space provided.

6. Describe mechanical digestion and chemical digestion.

_____

_____

7. Describe the three main parts of the nervous system and their functions.

_____

_____

_____

8. What is the difference between an antigen and an antibody?

_____

_____

9. What is the inflammatory response of the immune system?

_____

_____

10. Answer one of the following questions.
    a. Trace the path of food through the digestive system from the mouth to the large intestine.
    b. Draw a diagram or write a paragraph that describes how blood flows through the heart to the rest of the body.

Unit 1 TEST ANSWERS

1. endoplasmic reticulum   **2.** mitochondria   **3.** nucleus   **4.** cell membrane
5. ribosomes   **6.** Prokaryotic cells do not have a nucleus. Eukaryotic cells have a nucleus.   **7.** Mitochondria are organelles that supply the cell with energy.
8. The nucleus is the control center of a cell. It directs most of the activities that occur within the cell. The nucleus contains nucleic acids and nucleotides.   **9.** Active transport is the process in which energy is used to transport materials across the cell membrane. Passive transport is the movement of molecules across a cell membrane without the use of energy.   **10a.** Answers should include the following: nucleus: controls the cells activities, both; cell membrane: outer covering of the cell that controls the passage of substances into and out of the cell, both; cell wall: rigid structure that surrounds the cell membrane, plant cells; mitochondria: organelles that supply the cell with energy, both; cytoplasm: the living substance of a cell located between the nucleus and cell membrane, both; chromosomes: structures in the cell nucleus that control the passing of traits between generations, both; vacuoles: sacs that store food, wastes, and other materials, both; chloroplasts: organelles in which light energy is changed into chemical energy, plant cells; ribosomes: organelles at which proteins are made, both.   **10b.** Osmosis is the movement of water across a cell membrane. Water moves from an area of higher concentration to one of lower concentration. The concentration of water inside the cell is higher than that in the salted area outside the cell. Thus, water moves out of the cell into the area of lower concentration. The movement of water out of the cells kills the plant cells.

Unit 2 TEST ANSWERS

1. c   **2.** d   **3.** b   **4.** e   **5.** a   **6.** mRNA brings the code from the DNA to the ribosome. tRNA connects the amino acid with the mRNA at the ribosome.   **7.** A dominant gene is one that dominates, or masks, another gene for the same trait. A recessive gene is one that is not expressed when paired with a dominant gene.
8. Homozygous means an organism has two identical genes for a particular trait. Heterozygous means an organism has two different genes for a particular trait.   **9.** A chromosome mutation results when an error occurs as a chromosome copies itself. In this situation, the chromosomes in the resulting daughter cell are different from those of the parent cell.   **10a.** Half of the offspring would have bushy eyebrows and be heterozygous (Bb) for the dominant trait. Half of the offspring would have narrow eyebrows and be homozygous (bb) for the recessive trait.   Check students Punnett squares for accuracy.
10b. The number of amino acids allow for an enormous number of different combinations of amino acid chains to be built. This allows for the production of many different proteins. The traits of an organism are determined by its proteins. So, many different organisms can be created from the numerous protein combinations.

Unit 3 TEST ANSWERS

1. b   **2.** a   **3.** f   **4.** e   **5.** c   **6.** d   **7.** g   **8.** change or adapt   **9.** adaptation
10. survival of the fittest   **11.** species   **12.** genes   **13.** ancestors   **14.** 3 billion
15a. The early earth was covered with water and surrounded by an atmosphere made up of water vapor, hydrogen, ammonia, and methane. Violent thunderstorms were common.

Lightning from the storms provided energy to split the water molecules, and the elements in the molecules joined with carbon atoms to form small organic compounds. These organic compounds collected in shallow pools and eventually reacted with each other, forming larger compounds. The larger compounds began to act like cells and were the first living things on the earth.   **15b.** Ancestors are living species of the past from which other living species have evolved. Descendants are the living species that have evolved from ancestors.

Unit 4 TEST ANSWERS

1. vaccine **2.** decomposer **3.** bacteria **4.** Reproduction **5.** nitrogen-fixing bacteria
6. virus **7.** nucleus **8.** capsule **9.** blue-green bacteria **10.** flagellum **11.** paramecium
12. Cilia **13.** amoeba **14.** antibiotic **15a.** Helpful bacteria include decomposers that break down dead organisms, nitrogen-fixing bacteria that take nitrogen from the air and form useful compounds, and bacteria used in making foods such as yogurt. Harmful bacteria are those that cause food poisoning and diseases such as scarlet fever and tuberculosis **15b.** Labels on drawings will include cytoplasm, cell membrane, cell wall, capsule, and possibly a flagellum. Drawings should show a bacterium that is round, rod-shaped, or spiral.

Unit 5 TEST ANSWERS

1. vascular **2.** moss **3.** ovary **4.** seed **5.** gymnosperm **6.** angiosperms
7. photosynthesis **8.** flower **9.** Spores **10.** phloem **11.** fruit **12.** fern
13. Mosses are simple plants that do not have vascular tissue. Ferns are complex plants that have a vascular system. **14.** They have needle-shaped leaves with small surface areas that keep the plant from drying out. The leaves are protected by a hard, waxy coating that prevents water loss. **15a.** The plant would die. Without roots, the plant would not be able to take in water and nutrients. **15b.** The dye is placed in the plant's water supply. The stems of flowering plants contain the vascular tissue xylem that carries the dyed water to the rest of the plant, including the flower.

Unit 6 TEST ANSWERS

1. Asexual **2.** roundworm **3.** bivalve **4.** molt **5.** simple **6.** millipede
7. Tentacles **8.** mantle **9.** mollusk **10.** Radial **11.** cephalopod **12.** Tube feet
13.   Sponges are simple invertebrates that do not move and have saclike bodies with only one opening. Cnidarians are invertebrates that can move about and have a saclike body with a mouth surrounded by tentacles. **14.** The three main characteristics of arthropods are a segmented body, jointed legs, and an exoskeleton. **15a.** Flatworms feed on dead or slow-moving animals by secreting enzymes and partially digesting the food outside the body. The food is then brought into the body where it is further digested. Roundworms take in food through their mouths. Digested food is then absorbed from the digestive tube. Segmented worms, such as the earthworm, swallow soil that passes through the digestive system where the food is removed from the soil. **15b.** Answers will vary but may include the following: there would be fewer flowering plants because insects help

pollinate many different kinds of flowering plants, there might be less disease and damage caused by insects, there would be less beauty in the world because there would be no butterflies, there would be no honey from bees, and so forth.

Unit 7 TEST ANSWERS

1. mammal, hair   **2.** chordate, nerve   **3.** feathers, wings (in any order)   **4.** lungs **5.** Mucus   **6.** fishes, amphibians, reptiles, birds, mammals (in any order) **7.** endoskeleton   **8.** An endothermic animal is one whose internal body temperature stays constant regardless of the temperature of its environment. An ectothermic animal is one whose body temperature changes with the temperature of its environment. **9.** Internal fertilization takes place inside a female animal's body. External fertilization takes place outside a female animal's body, usually in water.   **10a.** Answers will vary but should include the following. Fishes live in water, breathe through gills, and have external fertilization. Reptiles live on land, breathe through lungs, and have internal fertilization. Reptiles have amniotic eggs that can be laid on land; fishes do not. **10b.** Vertebrates that live in water breathe through external gills and reproduce externally in the water. Vertebrates that live on land breathe with internal lungs, fertilize internally, and either have an amniotic egg or give birth to their young.

Unit 8 TEST ANSWERS

1. g   **2.** e   **3.** d   **4.** c   **5.** b   **6.** f   **7.** a   **8.** Commensalism and mutualism are two types of relationships among organisms within an ecosystem. Commensalism is a relationship in which one organism benefits and the other organism in unaffected. Mutualism is a relationship in which both organisms benefit. **9.** Producers are organisms that are able to make their own food. Consumers are organisms that obtain energy by eating other organisms: producers or consumers. Decomposers are organisms that obtain energy by breaking down dead organisms: either producers or consumers. **10a.** The rain forest biome receives more than 200 centimeters of rain each year and has warm temperatures. More species of plants and animals live in the rain forest biome than in any other biome. The deciduous forest biome receives more than 50 centimeters of rainfall per year and has warm summers and cold winters. The dominant plant life in this biome is deciduous trees. The taiga biome is characterized by forests of coniferous trees, warm summers, and long, cold, and dry winters.   **10b.** Answers should address viable ways of reducing air pollution (use public transportation, bike, etc.), reducing water pollution (do not dump chemicals, control use of fertilizers and pesticides, etc.), conservation of resources (recycle, use renewable instead of non-renewable resources, etc.), and so on. Accept all reasonable responses.

1. reproductive   **2.** muscular   **3.** skeletal   **4.** circulatory   **5.** respiratory
6. Mechanical digestion is the breaking down of food into smaller pieces by physical means. Chemical digestion is the breaking down of food into simple molecules by enzymes.
7. The three main parts of the nervous system are the brain, which serves as the control center of the body and makes the body react to all nervous impulses; the spinal cord, which connects the brain with the neurons in all parts of the body; and the nerves or neurons, which carry messages throughout the body.   **8.** An antigen is a foreign chemical on the surface of a pathogen. An antibody is a special protein produced by the immune system to fight off pathogens.   **9.** The inflammatory response is a process by which special white blood cells move from the blood into tissue where pathogens lie. The blood cells surround and destroy the pathogens.   **10a.** Food enters the mouth and is broken down into smaller pieces (mechanical digestion) by the teeth and mixed with saliva (chemical digestion). From there, the partly digested food enters the pharynx, passes through the muscular esophagus, and moves into the stomach. In the stomach, the food is turned into a thick liquid by both mechanical and chemical digestion. From the stomach, the food enters the small intestine, where most of the chemical digestion in the body takes place. Digested food is absorbed from the small intestine into the bloodstream. Undigested food and water pass from the small intestine to the large intestine where they are eliminated from the body.
10b. Diagrams or paragraphs should communicate the following. Deoxygenated blood from the body enters the heart at the right atrium. The blood then passes into the right ventricle and then through an artery to the lungs where it picks up oxygen. Oxygenated blood from the lungs enters the left atrium and then passes to the left ventricle. Oxygenated blood is pumped from the left ventricle to the rest of the body.